Ruby White

Michael O'Mara Humour

First published in Great Britain in 2000 by
Michael O'Mara Books Limited
9 Lion Yard, Tremadoc Road
London SW4 7NQ

A CIP catalogue record for this book is available from the British Library

ISBN 1-85479-560-0

1 3 5 7 9 10 8 6 4 2

Edited by David Brown
Designed and typeset by Design 23
Printed in China by Leo Paper Products Ltd

INTRODUCTION

Voodoo n. a national religious folk cult of Haiti involving witchcraft and communication by trance with ancestors and animistic deities.

To the uninitiated, various aspects of voodoo may seem shocking, bizarre or even strangely amusing. Following its sensational portrayal in numerous Hollywood movies since the 1930s, the word 'voodoo' has long conjured up a picture of scantily-clad young women being carted off into the jungle and forced to endure some unmentionable, bloodthirsty ritual at the hands of a crazed band of people with painted faces. Fortunately, the truth is somewhat different.

The Little Book of Voodoo aims to enlighten the unwise, inform the unknowing, and generally dispel some of the myths associated with this often misunderstood religion, as well as offering invaluable guidance on how to get the most out of voodoo in the twenty-first century, whether at home, in the office or on the move.

Remember, those who do ... use voodoo.

AFRICAN & HAITIAN ROOTS

The roots of voodoo go back to the West
African Yoruba people who lived in
eighteenth and nineteenth-century
Dahomey, a country that occupied parts of
today's Togo, Benin and Nigeria. Slaves
brought their religion with them when they
were forcibly shipped to Haiti and other
islands in the West Indies.

There are many alternative spellings for
voodoo, including *vodun, vodou, vodoun,
vaudou and vaudoux.* Each of these is an
attempt to spell the word in a way that
represents the Haitian pronunciation,

though in actual fact the word is rarely used by Haitians. They do not refer to the religion by the name voodoo, but speak of people 'following the *loa*' or 'serving the *loa*'. *Loa* or *lwa* means spirit.

In the Fon language spoken in the West African country of Benin, *vodun* means an invisible force, terrible and mysterious, which can meddle in human affairs at any time.

You remind me of a man
  What man?
  The man with a power
    What power?
    The power of Voodoo
      Voodoo?
      Voodoo
        Who do?
        You do!
          Do what?
          Remind me of a man
            What man?
            Etc…

7

As well as voodoo in Haiti, other religions that resulted from the slave trade are *candomblé* in Brazil, *santeria* in Cuba, *obeayisne* in Jamaica and *shango* cult in Trinidad. Two other religions similar to voodoo and found in South America are called *Umbanda* and *Quimbanda*.

Practising voodoo was made illegal in Haiti in 1835. It was not decriminalized until 1987.

Today over 60 million people throughout the world practice voodoo. It is followed by most of the adults in Haiti and by many people in the Dominican Republic and

Benin. It can be found in many of the large cities in the southern states of North America, usually where Haitian refugees have settled. When the French in Haiti realized that voodoo might be a threat to the colonial system, they forbade slaves to practise their native religions and baptized them as Catholics.

Slaves were automatically baptized into the Church upon their arrival in Haiti and other West Indian islands. However, as there was little Christian infrastructure present during the early nineteenth century the slaves largely followed original native faith, practising in secret, even while attending

Mass regularly. These worshippers also saw the addition of the saints as an enhancement of their voodoo faith, and they incorporated Catholic statues, candles and holy relics into their rituals.

VOODOO GODS

Legba is the Chief of the Spirit World.

Erzulie is the goddess of love, jealousy and vengeance.

Guede rules over the mysteries of death and of sorcery.

Baron Samedi is one of Guede's notorious helpers. He specifically watches over the graves.

Loa is used generically in reference to the major gods of voodoo.

Petro is a generic term for the minor and evil gods.

Rada is one of the names used to refer to all the good gods.

Simbi in Haitian voodoo are guardians of fountains and marshes. It is believed that children who go to fetch water at springs run the risk, particularly if they are fair skinned, of being abducted by a Simbi, who takes them under water to be his servants. After a few years he sends them back to the earth and, as a reward for their trouble, bestows upon them the gift of clairvoyance.

CAJUN VOODOO

Voodoo made its way to New Orleans from a variety of different places. Large numbers of slaves were imported to Louisiana directly from West Africa. There were also slaves from the French colonies of Guadeloupe, Martinique, and Santo Domingo. Many of the Haitian planters, as well as voodoo leaders, emigrated during the slave revolution of 1791. It is estimated that between 1805 and 1810, some 10,000 Caribbean refugees arrived in New Orleans.

In the early nineteenth century, exotic voodoo ceremonies, reported in lurid detail in the local newspapers, used to draw enormous throngs of thrill-seekers. But the ceremonies witnessed by the hordes and the reporters were usually elaborate shows staged for outsiders. In 1817, the New Orleans Municipal Council, fearful of voodoo-inspired slave uprisings, outlawed slave gatherings except on Sundays and in officially designated and supervised areas.

The first organized voodoo ceremony in New Orleans is said to have taken place in an abandoned brickyard on Dumaine Street. It was probably presided over by Sanite Dede, the first of the great voodoo queens. Repeated police raids on the brickyard drove the cultists out to Bayou St. John and Lake Pontchartrain.

VOODOO QUEEN

Voodoo was a matriarchy. The witch doctors and kings paled in comparison to the strong queens, always free women of colour, never slaves, who reigned over the rituals. In the early days of voodoo in New Orleans it seems that women made up at least 80 per cent of the followers. Amongst the white population it was always the women who entered the sect.

HOW DO YOU SOLVE A PROBLEM LIKE MARIE LAVEAU?

The greatest and most widely recognized voodoo queen of New Orleans was the famous Marie Laveau. She reigned as queen for over forty years. There are many conflicting stories about Madame Marie, whose life seems shrouded in mystery. Some accounts say she was born in 1794, others 1827. She is reputed to have returned the African custom of snake worship to New Orleans. Her *met tet*, or head spirit as referred to in voodoo, was Damballa, the great snake creator of voodoo mythology.

Marie was renowned for beating rivals as she came across them on the street and demanding that they relinquish their claims of superiority to her, in order to become the reigning voodoo queen. Much of Laveau's power, however, can probably be attributed to her great 'business' sense. Starting out as a hairdresser and gaining the respect and confidence of the New Orleans elite, she was able to use her knowledge of their secrets to carry out her public rituals undisturbed.

The early history of voodoo in New Orleans is peppered with exotic characters with names like Sanite Dede, Bayou John and Leafy Anderson.

VOODOO JOKE

It seems Hillary Clinton was making a public appearance in New Orleans and heard about a voodoo queen who could tell the future. So, Hillary crept away from the engagement and went down to talk to the fortune teller. 'I'd like to know what the future holds,' said Hillary. The voodoo queen gazed into her crystal ball and said, 'I'm sorry. I see a tragedy in your future. Your husband is going to be murdered.' Hillary took a deep breath, composed herself and said, 'Tell me. Will I be acquitted?'

VOODOO IN PRACTICE

Voodoo beliefs include:

The existence of a supreme being

An afterlife

A ritual sacrifice and the real or supposed
consumption of flesh and blood as
centrepoint of their ceremony

The existence of invisible evil spirits

Many voodoo believers still use the *mojo hand*, a small cloth filled with pieces of dead reptiles, birds, animals or even people, to 'fix' (hoodoo) someone or something. The most popular and potent *gris-gris* (lucky charm) is a root called 'Johnny the Conqueror'.

DOUBLE TROUBLE

Voodoo is of increasing interest in some schools of medicine and psychiatry in the southern states of America. Doctors in respectable medical schools have consulted voodoo doctors, especially with regard to the treatment of paranoid schizophrenics.

'A friend of mine is into Voodoo Acupuncture. You don't have to go to her office. You'll just be walking down the street and ... oohh, that's much better!'
Stephen Wright

VOODOO GLOSSARY

Asoto   Drum.

Asson   Rattle of the voodoo priest
              or priestess, symbol of
              spiritual power.

Bokor   A voodoo priest who uses
              sorcery.

Danse-loa   The 'fit of possession' in a
              voodoo ritual.

Dessouneu   Rite that separates the
                  'spirit' attached to an
                  initiate, just before or
                  after his or her death.

Gede   'Spirits' of the dead.

Govi   Pitcher containing the
                  'spirits'.

Gwo-bon anj   One of two spiritual
                  principles of the
                  individual, with *ti-bon
                  anj*.

Henga   Blood.

Loa   'Spirit' of the voodoo
                 religion; supernatural
                 beings that can enter the
                 human body, thought to be
                 present in all realms of
                 nature: earth, air, water, fire.
                 Loa establish a link
                 between human activities
                 and various aspects of the
                 natural world.

Loa-achte   Spirit purchased as
                 insurance against
                 misfortune.

Loa-met-tet   Protective spirit received at the time of initiation.

Mambo   Voodoo priestess.

Manje-loa   Sacrifice in a voodoo ritual.

Oufo   Voodoo temple.

Oungan
(or **boungan**)   Voodoo priest.

Ounsi   Voodoo initiate.

Peristyle   Open shed in the voodoo temple where the ritual dances take place.

Po-tet   Pot containing hair and nail clippings of a dead initiate.

Poteau-mitan Post in the centre of the peristyle that is the means by which the *loa* arrive amongst the humans.

Pwen   Supernatural power or magical protective force.

Ti-bon anj One of two spiritual principles of the individual, with *gwo-bon anj*.

Veve   Symbolic drawing of the *loa*.

Wanga   Evil charm.

BRING OUT YOUR DEAD!

One of the most important concepts in voodoo is the reverence for ancestor spirits. Voodoo practitioners believe that all of those who have come before you are important spirits and are worthy of tribute.

To create an ancestor altar: sit down and make a list of all your remembered relatives who have died. Then collect photographs of them and any items you have that may have belonged to them, to go on the altar. Also to be placed on the altar are the things that they enjoyed in life, such as beer, wine, whiskey, cigarettes and sweets. These items are not to be consumed by the living. Once they have been on the altar for a few days they should be removed, placed on the open earth and replaced with fresh items.

LORD OF THE TRANCE

The fundamental element of voodoo is the manifestation of the spirit world through the channel of a human being. It is necessary for the participant to be in a trance-like state to receive the spirits. This is induced by excitation brought on through the rhythm of dance, chanting and drums, especially the voodoo drum called a tamboula. Once in a trance the participant will not only be in touch with the spirits but also his or her unconscious, which will reveal secrets and guidance.

A typical voodoo ceremony has two main parts. First come the rites of entry; a parade of the oufo's flags; greetings to the sacred objects, including the drums; the rites of orientation of the sacred objects toward the four cardinal points to define the sacred space; and finally the invocations of the different *loa*, preceded by long Catholic prayers and the litanies of the saints. The air gradually warms from the dancing of the initiated to the rhythms of the drum around the *poteau-mitan.* Those who participate in the ceremony need to eat to recover their strength, the better to grant favours to their servants.

The second part of the ceremony features the sacrifice, known as the *manje-loa*. The ceremony is often directed by one or many worshippers who get together to buy the animals – goat, sheep, bull, or chicken – preferred by the *loa* from whom special favours are desired. Prepared dishes, such as grilled corn and cake, are left on the foot of the *poteau-mitan*, along with animals adorned with the colours of the *loa* to which they are being sacrificed.

TRADITIONAL VOODOO OFFERINGS FOR THE *LOA*

Papa Legba - cassava, rice, green bananas, smoked foods

Ezili - perfume, rice, chicken

Baron Samedi - salted herring, black hens

Simbi - black or grey animals

Damballah - all white foods, eggs

Les Gede - black goat or cockerel

Agwe - fine drink, champagne

Azaka - corn, bread, unrefined sugar

Ogou - cockerel

Aida Wedo - white foods, egg painted
rainbow colours

Traditional voodoo banners and flags are
an important and powerful part of the
voodoo religion. Their symbolic designs
are a synthesis of African, Roman Catholic,
Masonic and Arawak Indian influences.
The flags have a central role in voodoo
ritual. At the beginning of a ritual, the

flags are produced from a secret place, and are brought forward by apprentice voodoo priestesses, usually accompanied by machete-wielding assistants. The shimmering flags are waved in the candlelight to summon the *loas* to whom the ceremony is dedicated.

Any animals sacrificed at voodoo ceremonies are usually owned by the practitioners themselves; i.e. they are like pets and their sacrifice is unlikely to be taken lightly. Sacrificed animals are usually cooked and eaten afterwards. Fast food chicken outlets are probably responsible for the deaths of more chickens in one day than all the practitioners of voodoo in the past three hundred years.

The use of chicken feet is quite common in voodoo rituals. However the interpretation as to what their use actually symbolizes has varied over time and according to region. They have meant everything from keeping your mouth shut to good luck!

HOODOO VOODOO

Hoodoo (the 'fix') is a folk version of voodoo that focuses on conjuring and herbal magic. Some wouldn't equate voodoo with hoodoo, but hoodoo is a simplified version of the part of voodoo focusing on the magical. New Orleans voodoo is a bridge between Haitian voodoo and folk hoodoo. It still has religious and ritual elements like Haitian voodoo but also puts strong emphasis on gris-gris and magic.

ZOMBIE JOKES

**Do zombies eat popcorn
with their fingers?**
No, they eat their fingers separately!

**Why did the doctor tell the zombie
to get some rest?**
He was dead on his feet!

**Where do zombies play their
favourite game?**
On the golf corpse!

ZOMBIES!!!!

According to voodoo beliefs, a zombie is a dead body without a soul. Traditions state that a zombie can only be created by a black magician, or bokor, who carries out a death ritual. The bokor can then call the body back to life as a zombie. This seems unlikely; however, there does appear to be a basis in fact for the idea of zombies.

When the bokor performs the death ceremony, he anoints the person with a concoction of powerful ingredients, believed to contain extracts of hallucinogenic toad secretions, seeds and leaves from poisonous plants, and tetrodotoxin, which comes from puffer fish. The poisoned mixture is so deadly that the person often falls into a coma, and can appear to be dead. When the victim wakes after a period of time, which often includes an actual burial, he is usually so brain-damaged that he appears zombie-like. Without the qualities of an alert human being, the 'zombie' can be easily controlled and is often put to work as a slave to the bokor.

VOODOO IN POPULAR CULTURE

Hollywood's first movie about voodoo was *White Zombie*, made in 1932. This and the many subsequent Hollywood voodoo films established the 'satanic' image of the voodoo religion in the West and reinforced racist attitudes and negative stereotyping of black culture.

The idea that sex orgies are part of Haitian voodoo is a Hollywood fantasy. The only sex that takes place will probably be between young couples who slip away from the voodoo ceremony for some night-time fun and frolics on their own.

VOODOO MOVIES

Astro Zombies
Carnival of Souls
Dawn of the Dead
Day of the Dead
Dead Men Walk
The Fog
King of the Zombies
Midnight in the Garden of Good and Evil
Night of the Demons
Night of the Living Dead
Night of the Zombies
Plague of the Zombies
Return of the Living Dead
Revenge of the Zombies

Revolt of the Zombies
The Serpent and the Rainbow
Shock Waves
Voodoo Dawn
Voodoo Island
Voodoo Man
Voodoo Woman
I Walked With A Zombie
The Walking Dead
White Zombie
Zombies on Broadway
Zombie High
Zombie Island Massacre
Zombie Nightmare
Zombies of the Stratosphere
The Zombies of Sugar Hill

In a scene in one of the Hollywood voodoo films the Ritz Brothers walk up to a bar and say, 'Three zombies.' 'I can see that,' says the barman, 'but what'll you have to drink?'

The film *I Walked with a Zombie*, in which a doctor is sent to a Caribbean island to treat someone's zombie wife, is, unlikely as it might seem, based on the plot of *Jane Eyre*.

The Hollywood film *Zombie High* was retitled for its British release as *The School That Ate My Brain*.

In the second Austin Powers film, *The Spy Who Shagged Me*, Dr Evil has stolen Austin's *mojo*, and Austin has to get it back. Various famous people, including most famously, Jim Morrison of The Doors, have talked about a *mojo*, implying it is some sort of sexual spirit, or even something more basic. However, the word is probably derived from magic and refers to a mojo hand or bag, which is a receptacle for spells. The Doors' song, 'Mr Mojo Risin'', is simply an anagram of Jim Morrison.

MORE ZOMBIE JOKES

What goes ha ha splat?
A zombie laughing his head off!

How long can a zombie live?
      (a) About 50 years
      (b) About 150 years
      (c) About 500 years.
None - they're dead already!

Who did the zombie invite to his party?
Anyone he could dig up!

BAYOU BLUES

Dr. John, the famous blues singer (real name - Mac Rebenhack), took his name from *the* Doctor John, who was the most important male figure in the early New Orleans voodoo scene. Also known as Bayou John, he was a freed African slave who had travelled the world with his master. Descriptions depict him as a towering figure with a face tattooed with red and blue snakes, the tribal markings of the Senegalese royal family. He was widely sought by blacks and whites alike for his herbal medicines and fortune telling.

VOODOO SONGS

Voodoo Chile - Jimi Hendrix

Hootchie Kootchie Man &

I've Got My Mojo Working - Muddy Waters

Zombie - The Cranberries

Crawling King Snake Blues - John Lee Hooker

Love Voodoo - Duran Duran

I Put a Spell on You - Screamin' Jay Hawkins

In the Springtime of His Voodoo - Tori Amos

I'm a Man - Bo Diddley

Zombie Jamboree - recorded by various folk groups
As well as a band named The Zombies, The Rolling Stones
named an entire album and tour **Voodoo Lounge**

LIVIN' DOLLS

You can use almost anything to make a voodoo doll. Traditionally, voodooists have used materials indigenous to their area. In rural Louisiana, moss is used as stuffing, with sticks from local trees to form a cross as a base for the doll, around which they wrap the moss. Cotton or some other natural fabric is then wrapped around the base and the moss to create a head and 'clothes'. A personal item belonging to the individual one is trying to affect is often included in the filling.

The materials used to construct a voodoo doll are therefore as varied as the many regions in which the dolls were, and still are, constructed. You can see dolls of clay, cotton, mud, moss, straw, hair (animal and human), and combinations of these and many other materials, depending on where you are in the world.

The intended purpose of a voodoo doll affects the look of the doll and how it is made. For example, a fertility doll will often have exaggerations of the female form. Basically, the purpose of a doll can, and usually does, affect the maker's

choice of colour and the look and materials when they are creating a new doll.

These days you don't actually have to make your own doll - you can go out and buy one in a shop. In fact, you can buy a whole kit, complete with pins to stick in it.* However, if you have the time and the energy, it is much more satisfactory to make your own. If you are in a hurry, you can just make a quick doll shape out of play-dough or wax, but if you're feeling creative, this is how to do it.

*see page 95

HOW TO MAKE YOUR VERY OWN VOODOO DOLL

First of all, draw the shape of a person on to a piece of paper. You want your doll to be about fifteen centimetres long, so add an extra centimetre all the way round - this will allow you enough material to sew it up. Cut the shape out to give yourself a pattern from which to work.

Then take some white cotton - an old pillowcase or a piece of muslin will do - and fold it in half. Pin the pattern on to the fabric, and cut out the two shapes. Remove the pattern and sew the two pieces together, about one centimetre in from the edge, leaving a gap somewhere so that you can put the stuffing in. Now turn the fabric inside out, stuff the doll and sew it up.

You can use all sorts of things to stuff your doll – straw, grass, moss, cotton wool, cushion stuffing, tightly crumpled up newspaper – whatever comes to hand. You can add different herbs and spices to your stuffing, depending on what purpose the doll has. If it is a love doll, you could add red rose petals or orange blossom. If it is a revenge doll, you could try the green bits of potatoes, rhubarb leaves, dried stinkhorn mushrooms or, best of all, the flowers of Pelargonium Voodoo.

To make your doll as powerful as possible, try to add a little piece of your loved or loathed one. Collect fingernail clippings, stray hairs or even dandruff and add them to the stuffing. Try to make your doll look as much like the person you have in mind as possible - give it long hair or a moustache, draw in glasses or anything else that is appropriate. Now you are ready to begin.

PRECISION PIN TECHNIQUE

First of all you must concentrate on the person for whom you are making the doll, and hold their image in your mind as you insert the pin, while repeating your wish out loud. Use your common sense as to where to place the pin. For example, if you want to make someone love you, you could put a pin into the doll's heart area. If your lover is seeing someone else, you could put a pin between its legs. That should give him or her something to worry about!

If you want to **get rid of your boss**, try the following. If it is to be just for a week,

try a pin or two in their knees, or where
you think their appendix might be. If you
want them to go away for good, you could
try putting pins in all over the place.

You can try inserting the pins slowly, or
use a stabbing motion. If you feel like it,
you can twist it as it goes in. It just
depends on how you want the person to
feel the love or the pain. Keep the doll
close at hand, and tweak the pins now and
again during the day. If nothing happens,
try again, and next time, try a bit harder!

VOODOO RUMOURS

According to rumours on the internet, Bill Clinton consulted a voodoo practioner to ensure success in the presidential race, and, on his advice, did not change his underwear for the last week of the 1992 election campaign. He would have been performing a ritual known as a 'full week cycle', which uses an item of clothing that no one else is allowed to see, so the underwear is the only garment which could have been used in this case.

Voodoo is also said to have been used against George Bush. The same houngan who advised Clinton made a doll of the then President and manipulated it in order to make Bush have his unfortunate vomiting accident in front of the Japanese Prime Minister.

PRACTICAL VOODOO FOR EVERYDAY PEOPLE

Keep a doll in your bag, briefcase or pocket for those everyday situations where you can't think of a snappy reply in time, or where venting your anger quickly will be a whole heap more effective than biting your tongue.

If you want to get revenge on a **snooty assistant** who treated you like dirt in an exclusive shop, try a pin in the nose three times. Next time the – let's face it – shopgirl tries to look down her nose at you, all she will see is a great big boil!

To **silence the annoying commuter** who insists on singing along to his or her walkman, or talking loudly on his or her mobile, try pins in the ears of your doll.

When **the person in front of you in the cinema** is constantly in your way, no matter how you crane your neck, a pin in the bladder area of the doll will keep them in the loo and out of your way.

Sowing the seeds of love: add some couch grass to your doll when stuffing it. Then leave the doll in your bed for three days, before carrying it in your bag or pocket until you next see the object of your affection. When you meet your desired one, tug on the doll's arms three times, while visualising yourself in your beloved's embrace.

A hex on your ex: pull one arm of the doll forward, and the other arm backwards. Pin the hands together between the doll's legs. This should cause a certain amount of discomfort and irritation to delicate parts of your ex ...

Your cheatin' heart: if you suspect your partner of being unfaithful, but don't have any proof, will the doll to represent your partner and put a pin into the mouth area. Wrap the doll in an intimate item belonging to your partner, for example, a piece of underwear, handkerchief etc., and leave it in the dark for a week. After this time, if your partner is guilty, he or she will say something to prove their guilt.

When a teenage child is too unruly: to gain peace and quiet, wrap your voodoo doll completely in cotton wool and wind a length of red ribbon three times round to hold it in place. Hold the muffled voodoo doll up behind your child whenever they are being loud, and they will soon begin to leave you alone and modify their behaviour.

If you have an **interfering mother-in-law:** a drop of juniper juice in the mouth area will stop her nagging, and pins in the fingers will stop her rearranging your furniture, cutlery drawer, photograph albums etc.

A best friend's betrayal: if your best friend steals your boyfriend or girlfriend, your favourite outfit or never pays you back that money you lent them, you have a variety of punishment options. Pins in the hair will bring on premature baldness (only in patches); pins in the hands will cause them to lose their wallet or handbag, and pins in the feet will mean that they will get splashed by a car every time they walk past a puddle.

STICK IT TO THE SPICE GIRLS

If, in a moment of madness, you have bought some pop star dolls - Bay City Rollers, the Osmonds, even Barbie & Ken - you now have the perfect excuse to rid yourself of the annoying creatures. The Spice Girls work particularly well:

Baby – a pin in the pigtails will make them fall out

Scary – a pin in the throat will shut up her noxious whining

Posh – a pin in the pointy finger will stop her putting on that irritating pose again

Sporty – touch the pin to one of her tattoos, then stick it in anywhere you want more tattoos to appear

Ginger – a pin in the forehead will bring out her true age – Old Spice

HOW TO PROPERLY DISPOSE OF A CURSED VOODOO DOLL

On a Saturday, place the doll in a clean white cloth, dig a hole in the earth, far away from your home, on hallowed ground if possible, then place the cloth-wrapped doll in the hole and burn it. Next, cover the ashes which remain with holy water and cover over the hole with earth. The earth will recycle the negative energy very quickly and turn it into positivity and blessings. When you return home afterwards, bathe very well, adding some holy water to your bath.

VOODOO RITUALS

Spells and magic have been used successfully throughout history to accomplish a variety of goals. The effectiveness of every spell depends on several factors. Primarily, the responsibility for a spell's success or failure lies in the hands of the practitioner; it is your sheer will and desire to achieve the magical goal and your ability to creatively visualize and deeply focus on that goal that makes all the difference in the world.

In specialist shops in New Orleans you can buy voodoo ritual kits which contain everything you need to do your own voodoo ritual. Items in these kits include a coffin box, a voodoo doll, voodoo powders, a candle, some potion oil, a mini *gris-gris*, some parchment paper and incense.

One New Orleans voodoo specialist store requires that you specify the purpose when ordering one of their voodoo ritual kits. The purposes they offer include 'Unhexing', 'Win in Court', 'Enemy Be Gone' and 'Get That Job'. Among other voodoo accoutrements you can find in specialist shops in New Orleans are Love Oil, Courting Powder, Controlling Powder,

Get-Together Drops, Follow Me Drops and Boss Fix Powder.

Kyoto Powder, a classic voodoo powder mixture, is designed to provoke events. It is made up principally of absinte, patchouli and red sandalwood. Absinte is a plant derived from Mars which can only be combined with others derived from Venus to good effect. It will keep evil spirits at bay and encourage good luck. Patchouli, derived from Venus, burnt on Wednesday or Friday will attract new business propositions and love, and red sandalwood draws money harmony. The three mixed together in certain proportions cannot fail to bring good luck!

Most voodoo powders are intended to be burnt on live charcoal but in certain cases, such as the rather aptly named Money Drawing Powder, the mixture may be carried hidden about the person or tucked in places around the house.

SOME VOODOO POWDERS AND THEIR POWERS

Dragon Bath powder:
attracts great love and good luck.

Lady Luck powder:
attracts advice through dreams.

Mi-Gagne powder:
to have debts repaid and attract money.

Powder of protection:
to protect you during rituals and from accidents.

Invocation powder:
to call spirits and attract the paranormal.

Revenge powder:
purifies houses and expels evil.

Yo Yo powder:
keeps mistresses away from husbands.

VOODOO WITHOUT USING ACCESSORIES

To **keep your man sleeping** all night so you can play on his computer, wait until he falls asleep, then turn his shoes soles up, and cross them under the bed. Then, walk backwards out of the room.

To **ensure the success of your team** in sport, visit the pitch or ground where you will be playing at midnight two days beforehand, and walk around the outside of the playing area twice, backwards.

CURSE YOUR WAY TO SUCCESS

To make someone notice you, repeat the following lines daily for a week:

Papa Legba, show [insert the name of the person you want to notice you] *my face. Help him/her to recognise me and treat me as I deserve.*

To get revenge on a family member who has insulted you, chant these words for three days, facing the direction of his or her house, no matter how far away you live:

I call on Erzulie to help me regain my dignity, and to bring dishonour upon [insert the name of the relative] in even measure.

VOODOO PLANT SPELLS

Adder's Mouth
use to quiet a gossip: spread it on their
doorway.

African Ginger
use to protect against evil spirits and hexes:
spread around your house.

Angelica Root
place over the door to protect your house.

Anise
said to increase psychic abilities when
taken as a tea.

Brimstone
burn outside your home to dispel demons.

Buckeye
said to attract money to the business or home.

Catnip
place about the home for power and love.

Comfrey
said to protect the traveller.

Cowslip
place in a doorway to prevent unwanted visitors.

Couch grass

use to attract a new lover.

Dog grass

sprinkle on another's property to prevent
their happiness.

Fennel seed

carry to prevent negativity.

Flax

use in tea to enhance psychic abilities.

Holy Thistle

use to enhance spiritual help.

Hyssop
use for purification of any space.

Kava Kava root
protection while
travelling, protection
from accidents.

Lavender
use to promote love.

Peony root
use as a lucky charm.

Queen of the Meadow
bathe in it to see your future.

LOVE POTIONS

Attraction Oil: equal parts oils of rose, lavender, vanilla, and sandalwood. Touch to pulse points when in the presence of the one you want to attract.

Lucky Oil: $1/2$ of the oil should be pure olive oil, $1/4$ part oil of myrrh, $1/4$ part oil of jasmine. Anoint feet before putting on shoes you will wear in a situation where you want to feel lucky.

Power Oil: equal parts oils of patchouli, cinnamon and vanilla. Touch to pulse points (especially at wrists and temples) prior to going into a situation over which you need to have power.

Protection Oil: equal parts oils of hyacinth, jasmine, orange, musk and anise. Touch the oil around the area that needs protection (such as your home) or on yourself. It is claimed that touching this oil to the bottom of your feet allows you to run away from evil.

VOODOO CANDLES

Some voodooists are rather partial to burning special coloured candles to affect events or situations.

Green symbolizes: Nature, Money, Fertility, Abundance, Good Fortune, Co-operation, Generosity, Good Health, Renewal. Burning green candles promotes balance and harmony in any off-balance situation.

Pink symbolizes: Love, Honour, Togetherness, Gentleness, Spiritual Fulfillment. Pink candles may be burned for some healings, especially of the spirit. It is an excellent choice for domestic matters or 'true' love.

Purple symbolizes: Power, Royalty, Dignity, Wisdom, Idealism, Psychic Manifestation and Spirit Contact. Burning purple candles may be used effectively against Black Magic, demonic possession and for spiritual or psychic healing. It can also be used to throw up a veil of spiritual protection.

ZOMBIED!

There are several cocktails called
Zombies. The recipes vary according to
which Caribbean island they are from, and
even to the town in which they were
apparently first made. Thus there is a
Havana Zombie, a Port-au-Prince Zombie, a
Zombie Christophe and a Zombie Voodoo.
Essential ingredients for all Zombie
cocktails are two or three types of rum,
fresh fruit and plenty of ice.

Zombie Voodoo

Ingredients per glass:

5 ice cubes

Juice of one fresh lime or lemon

Juice of 1/2 fresh orange

3 drops Angostura bitters

1 teaspoon sugar or sugar syrup

1 egg white

1 part white rum

1 part gold rum

1 part dark rum

1 slice fresh orange

1 sprig fresh mint

1 maraschino cherry

Put the ice cubes into a cocktail shaker, pour the fruit juices over the cubes and shake the bitters into the shaker. Add the sugar, egg white, white and gold rum and shake until a frost forms. Pour without straining into a long glass, garnish with the fruit, top off with the dark rum, stir once and serve.

VOODOO SOUP

Serves four:

2 onions, chopped

4 cloves garlic, chopped

2 tablespoons olive oil

2 tablespoons plain flour

200 g/7 oz cooked kidney beans, drained

900 ml/1½ pints beef or vegetable stock

½-1 teaspoon curry powder, to taste

2 bay leaves

3 tablespoons peanut butter,
   crunchy or smooth

Large dash of vinegar-based hot pepper
   sauce, such as Tabasco

3 tablespoons chopped chives

1. Lightly sauté the onions and garlic in the olive oil. When softened and beginning to brown, stir in the flour and cook for several minutes, then add the beans and cook for a few more minutes.

2. Stir in the stock, curry powder and bay leaves, then bring to the boil. Reduce the heat and simmer over a medium heat for about ten minutes, or until the soup has thickened somewhat and smells enticing.

3. Remove the bay leaves and purée the beans in a food processor or liquidizer, adding enough liquid for a smooth texture. Return the purée to the stock,

then stir in the peanut butter.

4. Serve immediately, adding a dash of hot
pepper sauce and passing extra for the
other diners to add as they desire.
Sprinkle each portion with the chopped
chives.

Some other secret family recipes include
Jump the Broom Jambalaya, Mardi Gras
Marrying Gumbo, Please Me Now Pecan
Pie, Man Come With Me Soup, and Mister,
Stay Home Tonight Stew.

from *Cajun Voodoo Love Cookin'*
by Samantha Kaye and Hyacinth de la O

VOODOO JOKE

After a few years of married life while living in New Orleans, Jimmy finds that he is unable to perform anymore. He goes to the doctor and his doctor tries a few things but nothing seems to work. Finally his doctor refers him to a voodoo doctor. The voodoo doctor tells him 'I can fix this', and throws some powder on a flame, and there is a flash with billowing smoke. The voodoo doctor says, 'This is powerful healing, but you can only use it once a year! All you have to do is say "123" and it shall rise for as long as you wish!'

Jimmy asks the voodoo doctor, 'What happens when it's over?'

'All you have to say is "1234" and it will go down. But be warned, it will not work again for a year!'

Feeling very good about himself, Jimmy goes home and that night he is ready to surprise his wife with the good news. So, he is lying in bed with her and says, '123', and suddenly he gets an erection. His wife turns over and says, 'What did you say "123" for?'

Now you have read this little book, you too can have the power to take control of your life. With a voodoo doll in your pocket, you never have to raise a hand in anger again - simply pop in a pin and extract your revenge.

Remember, you can create your own curses and rituals, as long as you use the force of your will as the main ingredient. Take care to speak the truth and you will have a long and healthy voodoo career.

VOODOO IS FOR YOU!